United States. mn Northwest Territory

Laws passed in the territory of the United States north-west of the river Ohio

from July to December

United States. mn Northwest Territory

Laws passed in the territory of the United States north-west of the river Ohio
from July to December

ISBN/EAN: 9783337374471

Printed in Europe, USA, Canada, Australia, Japan

Cover: Foto ©ninafisch / pixelio.de

More available books at **www.hansebooks.com**

LAWS

PASSED IN THE

TERRITORY

OF THE

UNITED STATES

NORTH-WEST

OF THE

RIVER OHIO,

FROM

JULY TO DECEMBER,

ONE THOUSAND SEVEN HUNDRED AND NINETY-TWO, INCLUSIVE.

Published by Authority

PHILADELPHIA:

PRINTED BY FRANCIS CHILDS AND JOHN SWAINE,
Printers of the Laws of the United States.

M.DCC.XCIV.

A COPY of Laws paſſed in the Territory of the United States North-Weſt of the River Ohio, from July to December, 1792, incluſive.

WINTHROP SARGENT.

The PRESIDENT *of the* United States.

DEPARTMENT OF STATE, *to wit.*

I hereby certify, that the foregoing "Copy of laws passed in the Territory of the United States, North-west of the river Ohio, from July to December, 1792, inclusive," has been carefully collated with, and rendered literally conformable to the original, on file in the office of the Department of State.

GEO. TAYLOR, *jr. Chief Clerk.*

20 *January*, 1794.

Page.

AN act for granting licenses to merchants, traders and tavern-keepers - - - - 5

An act creating the offices of treasurer-general of the territory and treasurers for the counties - 13

An act directing the manner in which money shall be raised and levied, to defray the charges which may arise within the several counties in the territory - - - - - - - 16

An act for opening and regulating high ways - 21

An act directing the building and establishing of a court-house, county jail, pillory, whipping-post and stocks, in every county - - - 26

An act for the better regulation of prisons - 29

An act for the disposition of strays - - - 35

An act to repeal certain parts of an act, entitled, an act "creating the office of clerk of the legislature" - - - - - - - 39

An act supplementary to a law, entitled, a "law regulating marriages" - - - - *ibid*

An act to regulate the admission of attornies - 40

An act empowering the judge of probate to appoint guardians to minors and others - - 41

An act prescribing forms of writs in civil causes, and directing the mode of proceeding therein 46

An act establishing and regulating the fees of the several officers and other persons therein mentioned - - - - - - - 57

CHAPTER I.

An ACT *for granting Licenses to Merchants Traders and Tavern-keepers passed at Cincinnati in the county of Hamilton and Territory of the United States north-west of the river Ohio the first day of August in the year of our Lord one thousand seven hundred and ninety-two by* Winthrop Sargent *Secretary and now vested with all the powers of the Governor and* John Cleeves Symmes *and* Rufus Putnam *Judges.*

Sec. 1. BE *it enacted* That if any person or persons shall presume to set up or open a store for the sale of merchandize consisting of dry goods or of articles in the grocery way which are not of the growth production or manufacture of some part of the United States or of one of their territories or shall presume to expose directly or indirectly any such articles or things for sale within the said territory and if any person or persons shall presume to sell or vend any whiskey geneva cordials strong waters or ardent spirits of any kind although the same may be of the manufacture of some part of the United States or of one of their territories in a smaller or less quantity than ten gallons except such person or persons be first duly licensed for the purpose as is herein after directed he she or they so offending shall forfeit and pay five dollars with costs of suit for each and every sale or transfer of goods or other articles actually made one half of which penalty shall go to the person who will sue therefor in any court where the same may be cognizable and prove the fact by the testimony of a third person and the other half to the use of the county in which the offence shall be committed. Provided that when the offence is proved by the oath of the party complain-

Penalty on selling goods or ardent spirits without license;

how to be recovered and disposed of.

ing the whole penalty ſhall be for the uſe of the county.

Commiſſioners for granting licenſes to be appointed in each county;

Sec. 2. *And be it further enacted* That one or more commiſſioners ſhall be appointed by the governour in each and every county whoſe title ſhall be "Commiſſioner for granting Licenſes" and duty ſhall be ſeverally and they are hereby authoriſed and required each under his hand and ſeal to grant a licenſe which ſhall run for the term of one year only from its date to any and every perſon mercantile houſe or firm applying for the ſame for the purpoſe of opening a ſtore or of expoſing goods or other articles as aforeſaid to ſale in the county in which application is made on ſuch perſon, mercantile houſe or firm paying therefor ſixteen dollars fifteen of which ſhall be for the uſe of the county and each commiſſioner granting a licenſe ſhall forthwith pay the fees thereof as aforeſaid to the treaſurer of the county for the time being taking his receipt therefor and the reſidue of one dollar in every inſtance the commiſſioner ſhall retain as a reward for his ſervices herein and he ſhall within thirty days after granting ſuch licenſe lodge a copy thereof with the clerk of the ſeſſions on penalty of paying a fine of ſixteen dollars for each neglect to the uſe of the county to be recovered at the ſuit of the treaſurer of the county in any court proper to try the ſame with coſts of ſuit. And the clerk ſhall regiſter the name of the perſon and date of the licenſe and file the copy in his office.

term of [illegible];

ſum to be paid for [illegible] licenſe; how [illegible] [illegible];

copy of licenſe [illegible] and where lodged.

Commiſſioners to enter licenſes in a book.

And each and every commiſſioner reſpectively ſhall keep fair entries in a book by him provided for the purpoſe of all licenſes as aforeſaid their ſeveral dates and to whom iſſued and in the ſame book he ſhall charge himſelf as debtor to the county fifteen dollars for every ſuch licenſe crediting himſelf alſo with the monies by him paid from time to time to the said treasurer of the county. And once in every year some time in the month of December the commissioner shall lodge with the clerk of the sessions a fair account of his receipts and payments of such license money and whenever required thereto by the Court of General Quarter Sessions shall exhibit his books of entries kept as aforesaid for their examination on penalty of paying a fine of ninety dollars for each neglect to the use of the county to be recovered at the suit of the treasurer in manner aforesaid. And each and every person mercantile house or firm, suing out license as aforesaid shall cause to be set up on some conspicuous part of the front and outside next the street of his store shop or place of sales for the information of the public a board or sign on which shall be written in large fair letters "By authority a licensed store"

Commissioner when and where to settle accounts.

Duty of persons suing out license.

Sec. 3. *And be it enacted* That if any person shall presume to be an inn-holder a tavern-keeper retailer or seller of wine brandy rum geneva whiskey or ardent spirits or liquors mixed or unmixed in a less quantity than one quart and that delivered and carried away from the house or place of sale all in one vessel at one time so that it be not drank at all at the place or tenement where sold nor on the appurtenances belonging thereto except such person be duly licensed as herein after is directed he or she so offending shall forfeit and pay five dollars with costs of suit for every such offence one half of which penalty shall go to the person who will sue therefor in any court where the same may be cognizable and prove the offence by the testimony of a third person and the other half to the use of the county in which the offence shall be committed. But when the

Penalty on retailing less than a quart of liquor, &c.

how disposed of.

offénce is proved by the oath of the perſon complaining the whole penalty ſhall be for the uſe of the county.

Power of commiſſioners herein.

Sec. 4. *And be it enacted* That the commiſſioner for granting licenſes ſhall have a power of eſtabliſhing public inns and taverns and alſo retailers of ſpirituous liquors and they are hereby ſeverally authorized any one of them to grant licenſes for the purpoſe under his hand and ſeal to ſuch perſon or perſons as the juſtices of the General Quarter Seſſions of the Peace in their wiſdom may deem really neceſſary well qualified in perſon and character well provided in accommodations for gueſts and well ſituate in point of reſidence for the accommodation of travellers and citizens and the convenience comfort and uſe of the public and certified to the commiſſioner under the hand of the clerk of the ſaid court.

May grant licenſes for inns on certificate of juſtices,

Sec. 5. *And be it enacted* That the commiſſioner whenever the juſtices at their General Seſſions of the Peace ſhall recommend for the purpoſe may make out a licenſe under his hand and ſeal to ſuch perſon or perſons in whoſe favour the certificate of the court may be made tolerating and appointing him her or them to commence and keep for the term of one year and no longer from the date thereof a public inn tavern or houſe for retailing of ſtrong liquors in ſuch place within the county as ſhall be mentioned by the court in their certificate the perſon or perſons ſuing out the licenſe previouſly paying therefor unto the commiſſioner ſixteen dollars fifteen of which ſhall be for the uſe of the county and the commiſſioner ſhall forthwith pay the ſame to the treaſurer of the county for the time being taking his receipt therefor and the remaining one dollar ſhall be the fee of the commiſſioner for his ſervices

for one year only;

for what ſum;

to be paid over to county treaſurer.

herein. And the commiſſioner ſhall keep fair entries in a book by him provided for the purpoſe of all licenſes as aforeſaid their ſeveral dates and to whom iſſued and in the ſame book ſhall charge himſelf as debtor to the county fifteen dollars for every ſuch licenſe crediting himſelf alſo with the monies paid by him from time to time to the ſaid treaſurer of the county. And each and every perſon obtaining licenſe from the commiſſioner as aforeſaid ſhall ſet up in a proper manner on the front and outſide of his houſe next the ſtreet a board or ſign with his or her name written thereon and ſome device expreſſive of his buſineſs as a tavern-keeper or retailer of liquors on which board or ſign ſhall alſo be written in large fair letters "By authority a tavern." or By "authority a retailer" as the caſe may be. And the commiſſioner ſhall within thirty days after granting ſuch licenſe lodge a copy thereof with the clerk of the ſeſſions on penalty of paying a fine of ſixteen dollars for each neglect to the uſe of the county to be recovered at the ſuit of the treaſurer of the county in any court proper to try the ſame with the coſts of ſuit and the clerk ſhall regiſter the name of the perſon and date of the licenſe and file the copy in his office and once in every year ſome time in the month of December the commiſſioner ſhall lodge with the clerk of the ſeſſions a fair account of his receipts and payments of ſuch licenſe money and whenever required thereunto by the Court of General Quarter Seſſions ſhall exhibit his books of entries kept as aforeſaid for their examination on penalty of paying a fine of ninety dollars for each neglect to the uſe of the county to be recovered at the ſuit of the treaſurer in manner aforeſaid.

Commiſſioner to enter the ſame in a book.

Duty of perſons obtaining licenſes for inns, &c.

Copy of licenſe where lodged;

penalty on neglect thereof.

Accounts when to be ſettled;

penalty on neglect thereof.

[illegible] *Sec. 6. And be it further enacted* That if any perſon licenſed to keep a public inn or tavern as aforeſaid ſhall neglect or refuſe to do his or her duty therein as well in providing good and wholeſome food for man and beaſt as in keeping ordinary liquors of a good and ſalutary quality and ſuitable lodgings and attendance for gueſts in a reaſonable and proper manner according to the common uſage and cuſtom of well kept taverns in an inland country it ſhall and may be lawful for any one or more of the juſtices of the peace the ſheriff deputy ſheriff and conſtables in the county and it is hereby enjoined on and made the duty of each and every of them ſeverally as far as may at any time come to their knowledge and obſervation officially to report and make known any evil practice connivance at unlawful gaming or neglect of duty as aforeſaid in a tavern-keeper inn-holder or retailer of ſtrong liquors to the juſtices of the Court of General Quarter Seſſions of the Peace at their next enſuing ſeſſions after ſuch offence or neglect committed which report or complaint ſhall be entered on the records and read in open court and ſhall be ſufficient ground and evidence whereon the court may proceed two days afterwards to revoke and annul the licenſe granted for the time being to the perſon or perſons complained of unleſs the perſon ſo complained of ſhall of his or her own motion come into court with two good and ſufficient ſureties who with him or her ſhall ſubmit to be bound in recognizance the tavern-keeper in the ſum of one hundred dollars and the ſureties in the ſum of fifty dollars each conditioned that ſuch principal or tavern-keeper during the reſidue of the term of his or her licenſe ſhall keep and maintain good rule and order in his or her houſe not ſuffering games of any kind contrary to the laws of

and inn-keepers [illegible] give [illegible] keeping orderly [illegible] the territory to be played therein nor in any of the dependencies thereof and in all things acquit himſelf herſelf or themſelves with propriety and caution as a tavern-keeper or retailer of liquors of good acceptance and repute with the public ought to do according to the laws of the territory. And on default being made in the recognizance aforeſaid the attorney proſecuting the pleas of the United States for the county ſhall bring a ſcire facias thereon in the county Court of Common Pleas held for the county and proſecute the ſame with coſts to judgment and execution in the uſual form according to the practice of the ſaid court and the money after being levied by the ſheriff ſhall be by him paid to the treaſurer of the county for the uſe of ſuch county.

on default how proceeded.

Sec. 7. *And be it further enacted* That if any inn-holder or tavern-keeper ſhall refuſe to receive refreſh and entertain with ſuitable proviſion and accommodation if required thereto any ſtranger traveller or other perſon or perſons appearing to be of ability to make ſatisfaction for the ſame and in the peace of the United States the tavern-keeper ſo offending ſhall be ſubject to the action of ſuch ſtranger traveller or other perſon for any damages he ſhe or they may have ſuſtained in conſequence of ſuch refuſal neglect or inattention to be recovered with coſts in any court where the ſame may be cognizable.

Inn-keepers refuſing to entertain travellers,

how proſecuted,

Sec. 8. *And be it further enacted* That no keeper or keepers of a tavern public inn or houſe for retailing of ſtrong liquors ſhall ſupport any action for or be allowed any bill or charge over and above a balance of two dollars in any ſuit action demand or proſecution in law by book note of hand or ſpecialty againſt any perſon living within five miles of ſuch ta-

and in what caſes not allowed action for more than two dollars.

vern public inn or houſe for retailing of ſtrong liquors by a ſmaller quantity than one quart at the time when ſuch debt or demand accrued where the conſideration of the debt or demand ſhall appear to the court to have ariſen after the publication of this act and to be for any article or articles ſold or furniſhed to or for the uſe of any perſon in the character of gueſts or cuſtomers at ſuch tavern inn or houſe for retailing of ſtrong liquors by the keeper or keepers thereof in the line or way of his her or their profeſſion. And where the balance of the whole demand or charges collectively taken ſhall exceed two dollars then in ſuch caſe for ſo much of the demand as ſhall appear to be above the ſaid ſum or balance of two dollars a non-ſuit operating in the nature of a releaſe in favour of the defendant ſhall be entered by the court or magiſtrate before whom ſuch action ſhall be brought and ſuch releaſe ſhall be juſtified by force of this act and the court ſhall give judgment for two dollars only.

This act when to take effect.

Sec. 9. *And be it enacted* That this act ſhall commence and be in force from and immediately after the firſt General Seſſions of the Peace which may be held in the ſeveral counties reſpectively after the publication thereof in ſuch county.

Signed
WINTHROP SARGENT,
JOHN CLEVES SYMMES,
RUFUS PUTNAM.

CHAPTER II.

An ACT *creating the Offices of Treasurer General of the Territory and Treasurers for the Counties passed at Cincinnati in the county of Hamilton the first day of August in the year of our Lord one thousand seven hundred and ninety-two by* Winthrop Sargent *Secretary vested with all the powers of the Governour in the absence of the Governour of the Territory north west of the river Ohio and* John Cleves Symmes *and* Rufus Putnam *Judges of the same.*

Sec. 1. BE *it enacted* That there shall be appointed and commissioned during pleasure an officer to be stiled Treasurer-General of the Territory. Establishment of general treasurer;

Sec. 2. It shall be his duty to receive and keep in the treasury of the territory for the use of this territory all dues fines amercements forfeitures revenues and emoluments which are or may hereafter be due given coming or accruing to the use and benefit of the territory according to the ordinances laws rules regulations or government thereof. his duty

Sec. 3. He shall from time to time pay and appropriate such sum or sums of money as may come to his hands as treasurer in the manner and form and on such occasions as are or shall be by law directed. And for the faithful discharge of his duty as treasurer-general he shall enter into bond to the governour of the territory for the time being with two sufficient sureties in the penal sum of four thousand dollars. And the said treasurer shall be entitled to retain for his own use out of the public monies as the same shall come to his hand a sum after the rate of five per centum in full compensation for his services and all expences incident to his office. allowance;

Sec. 4. The said treasurer shall have power and he is hereby authorized to demand of and to sue and prosecute to judgment and effect by power;

power of general treasurer; means of the attorney prosecuting the pleas of the United States (except where suit or prosecution shall have been previously instituted by the attorney-general) any person or persons having in possession and neglecting to pay the same when due and owing to the territory any sum or sums of money accruing to or received for the use thereof. And for this purpose the treasurer-general shall be furnished by the clerks of the several courts of justice respectively once in every year with authenticated extracts from the records and dockets of their respective courts of all forfeitures fines amercements escheats judgments and orders entered in such courts whereby monies may be arising or accruing to the use of the territory and if any clerk as aforesaid shall neglect his duty herein he shall be liable to pay a fine to the use of the territory in the discretion of the court where tried not exceeding one hundred dollars to be levied on complaint of the treasurer-general or of the attorney prosecuting the pleas of the United States in the county and conviction thereon had in the Supreme Judicial Court of the territory or in the Court of General Quarter Sessions of the Peace in the respective counties.

to keep fair books; Sec. 5. The said treasurer shall keep fair and proper books of entries and accounts of all monies which may have come to his hands as treasurer-general and also of all monies by him paid out of the general treasury to whom and to what purpose paid and he shall lay the same books and accounts before the legislature of the territory and settle with that body his accounts as often as he shall be thereunto required. with whom and when to settle accounts.

County treasurers to be appointed; Sec. 6. *And be it also enacted* That there shall be appointed and commissioned in and for each and every county in the territory an officer to be ſtiled the County Treaſurer.

Sec. 7. It ſhall be his duty to receive and keep for the uſe of the county of the proper perſons who ought to pay the ſame all monies due and owing at any time to the county or accruing to the uſe thereof. He ſhall pay or cauſe to be paid the ſame monies or ſuch part thereof as may come to his hands in the manner and to the purpoſes directed by law. And for the faithful diſcharge of the truſt and duties hereby enjoined on him the ſaid county treaſurer ſhall give bond with two ſufficient ſureties to the governour for the time being in the ſum of one thouſand five hundred dollars. their duty; to give bond;

Sec. 8. And each county treaſurer by means of the attorney-general or perſon officiating as ſuch in his county ſhall have power and he is hereby authoriſed to enforce the payment of all dues fines amercements forfeitures revenues and emoluments which are or may hereafter be due given coming or accruing to the uſe of the county in the ſame manner as the treaſurer-general is by this act authoriſed to do in reſpect of monies due or accruing to the uſe of this territory. their power;

Sec. 9. He ſhall annually lay before the legiſlature of the territory an account of all monies that ſhall have been raiſed in the county to which he belongs by aſſeſſment or by any other way or means by him received as county treaſurer and how the ſame has been diſpoſed of. And no further aſſeſſment ſhall be made on the ſeveral towns and places in the county to which he belongs until the ſaid amount has been offered to the legiſlature and allowed by them. with whom and when to ſettle.

County treasurer's allowance.

Sec. 10. As a compensation for all services and expences incidental to his office the said county treasurer shall and may retain for his own use out of all the public monies as the same shall come to his hands a sum after the rate of five per centum.

Signed
WINTHROP SARGENT
JOHN CLEVES SYMMES
RUFUS PUTNAM.

CHAPTER III.

An ACT *directing the manner in which Money shall be raised and levied to defray the Charges which may arise within the several Counties in the Territory passed at Cincinnati the first day of August in the year of our Lord one thousand seven hundred and ninety-two by* Winthrop Sargent *Secretary and now vested with all the powers of the Governour of the Territory north-west of the river Ohio and* John Cleves Symmes *and* Rufus Putnam *Judges.*

Courts to estimate expenses of counties;

Sec. 1. BE *it enacted* That the Court of General Quarter Sessions of the Peace at the last term which shall be held within each of the counties next preceding the first day of January annually shall make an estimate of such sum or sums of money as they according to their best skill and judgment shall think sufficient to defray the necessary charges of their respective counties for one year specifying as nearly as may be the purposes for which such sum or sums may be necessary and which may properly be considered as county charges which estimate the clerk of the said court is hereby directed to lay before the governour and two or more of the judges of the territory from time to time as soon as may be after such estimate shall have been formed so that such sum as may be necessary for the purposes aforesaid and approved of by the legislature may be laid on the inhabitants of each county respectively.

to be laid before the governor, &c.

Sec. 2. *And be it enacted* That the ſums which ſhall from time to time be allowed by the legiſlature and laid on the ſeveral counties for the purpoſes aforeſaid ſhall be apportioned on the inhabitants of the ſeveral towns or diſtricts within the reſpective counties by commiſſioners annually to be appointed by the judges of the Court of Common Pleas and the number of ſaid commiſſioners ſhall be aſcertained by the following rule. In every town or diſtrict one commiſſioner ſhall be appointed and when any town or diſtrict ſhall conſiſt of ſixty male inhabitants of twenty one years of age and upwards they ſhall have two commiſſioners and if of one hundred ſuch inhabitants or more they ſhall have three commiſſioners. And the ſaid commiſſioners when appointed ſhall meet at a time and place to be aſcertained by the ſaid judges of the Court of Common Pleas and proceed to apportion the ſaid ſum or ſums to be allowed by the legiſlature on the inhabitants of the ſaid towns or diſtricts within the reſpective counties as aforeſaid in which apportionment the ſaid commiſſioners ſhall have ſpecial reſpect to wealth and numbers and may direct the whole aſſeſſment to be made in money or ſpecific articles moſt agreeable with the neceſſity of the public and convenience of the people. And the better to enable the commiſſioners to make ſuch apportionment conſiſtent with equity and the abilities of the people they are hereby empowered to take a liſt of the male inhabitants from eighteen years old and upwards with ſtocks of cattle yearly value of improved lands and every other ſpecies of property which may be in the county and ought to affect the apportionment. how apportioned.

Sec. 3. *And be it further enacted* That the ſaid judges of the Court of Common Pleas in Judges to appoint aſſeſſors.

Judges may appoint assessors; each county respectively may and they are hereby authorised and required annually to appoint in each township village or district three judicious men two of whom shall have power to assess and apportion on the inhabitants of their respective towns villages and districts for which they may be appointed assessors the sum or sums which by order of the commissioners is directed to be assessed on the inhabitants of such town village or district.

their powers;

Sec. 4. And the said assessors in making any assessment by virtue of this law shall assess the individuals of their town village or district according to the best of their judgment in just proportion to their wealth in the county and ability to pay either in money or specific articles agreeably to the order of assessment they shall receive from the commissioners and all assessors appointed as aforesaid shall severally take the following oath before one of the justices of the peace in the county viz. "I do solemnly and sincerely swear (or affirm as the case may be) that I will to the best of my judgment and information impartially and faithfully execute the office of assessor in the township of agreeably to law and justice so help me God."

to take oath.

Term of appointments hereto.

Sec. 5. *And be it further enacted* That all appointments of commissioners and assessors under this law shall be for one year only and any person not being an officer of the territory appointed assessor refusing to take the oath or affirmation and do the duties of his appointment shall pay a fine of twenty dollars for the use of the county where he belongs and the said judges shall appoint another in his stead. Provided that no man shall be compelled to serve as assessor more than one year in three.

Sec. 6. *And be it further enacted* That within the time limited by the order of affeffment the affeffors of each townfhip village or diftrict fhall lodge with the prothonotary of the Court of Common Pleas a lift of the affeffment by them made in purfuance of fuch order of affeffment under their hands and feals on penalty of paying a fine not exceeding fifty dollars each to the ufe of the county. And the prothonotary fhall from the affeffor's lift lodged as aforefaid make out a duplicate thereof with a warrant of diftrefs under his hand and the feal of the court directed to the fheriff or conftable or to fuch other perfon as the Court of Common Pleas fhall appoint requiring him to collect and pay the fame to the treafurer of the county for the ufe of the county as aforefaid.

Duty of affeffors.

Duty of prothonotary.

Sec. 7. *And be it further enacted* That if any perfon fhall refufe to pay the fum or fums which he fhall be affeffed as his proportion of any rate or affeffment laid as aforefaid (to defray the expenfes of the county to which he belongs) in the lift or duplicate committed to any fheriff conftable or collector by virtue of the warrant to him given it fhall and may be lawful for fuch fheriff conftable or collector and he is hereby authorifed and required in fuch cafe to diftrain the perfon fo refufing by his goods or chattels and the diftrefs fo taken to keep for the fpace of four days at the coft and charges of the owner thereof and if the owner do not pay the fum or fums of money fo affeffed on him (or if the tax be in fpecific articles he do not deliver or tender the fame at the place affigned) within the fpace of four days then the faid diftrefs fhall be openly fold at public auction by the faid officer for the payment of the faid money notice of fuch fale being fet up in fome public place in the fame

Proceedings to be had againft perfons refufing to pay tax.

Proceedings to be had againſt perſons refuſing to pay tax.

town village or diſtrict forty-eight hours before the ſale and after the expiration of the four days aforeſaid.' And the overplus ariſing by ſuch ſale if any over and above the charges of taking and keeping the ſaid diſtreſs to be immediately returned to the owner with an account in writing of the ſale and charges thereon.

In what caſes the body may be taken.

Sec. 8. *And be it alſo enacted* That if any perſon aſſeſſed as aforeſaid ſhall refuſe or neglect to pay the ſum or ſums ſo aſſeſſed for the ſpace of twelve days after demand thereof being made and ſhall alſo neglect to ſhew to the officer ſufficient goods or chattels whereon diſtreſs may be levied in every ſuch caſe the officer may take the body of the perſon ſo refuſing into his cuſtody and him commit to the common jail of the county there to remain until the ſame be paid or he be thence delivered by due order of law. And the keeper of the jail in the ſeveral counties is hereby authoriſed and required to receive ſuch delinquent into the common jail as aforeſaid. Provided nevertheleſs that in all caſes where in the opinion of two or more juſtices of the peace there is juſt ground to fear that any perſon or perſons aſſeſſed as aforeſaid may abſcond before the expiration of the ſaid twelve days in ſuch caſe it ſhall be in the power of the ſheriff conſtable or collector to demand immediate payment and proceed as is heretofore directed.

Perſons unequally taxed how to proceed.

Sec. 9. *Provided always and be it further enacted* That if any perſon or the inhabitants of any town village or diſtrict ſhall think himſelf or themſelves unequally or unreaſonably aſſeſſed if the inhabitants of a town village or diſtrict they may by petition apply to the judges of the General Court judges of the Court of Common Pleas in the county where ſuch town village or diſtrict lies or juſtices of the court of General Quarter Seſſions of the Peace who are hereby empowered in their ſeveral courts to abate or remit the ſum in which the complainants are aſſeſſed or which was apportioned on them or ſuch part thereof as they ſhall judge ought to be abated or remitted and an order of the Supreme Judicial Court of the Court of Common Pleas or of the Court of General Quarter Seſſions of the Peace ſhall be a ſufficient warrant to the treaſurer of the county to diſcount or repay the ſame. And if the complaint be againſt the aſſeſſors for the unequal aſſeſſment of individuals they may petition the judges of the Supreme Court the judges of the Court of Common Pleas or the juſtices of the Court of General Quarter Seſſions of the Peace who are hereby empowered in their reſpective courts to redreſs the grievances complained of if any exiſt and the perſon in whoſe hands the money or ſpecific articles may be which are ſo remitted or abated ſhall reſtore the ſame to the perſon in whoſe favor redreſs is allowed on the order of either of the aforeſaid courts.

Signed WINTHROP SARGENT
JOHN CLEVES SYMMES
RUFUS PUTNAM.

CHAPTER IV.

An ACT *for opening and regulating High Ways paſſed at Cincinnati in the county of Hamilton the firſt day of Auguſt in the year of our Lord one thouſand ſeven hundred and ninety-two by* Winthrop Sargent *Secretary now veſted with all the powers of the Governour and* John Cleves Symmes *and* Rufus Putnam *Judges.*

Sec. 1. BE *it enacted* That whenever a petition ſigned by twelve or more citizens dwelling within any county in the territory ſhall be preſented to the juſtices ſpecially

Proceedings to be had for opening high-ways &c

Proceedings to be had for opening high-ways.

named in the commiſſion for holding the court of General Quarter Seſſions of the Peace for ſuch county while in ſeſſion praying the ſaid court to order a public high-way to be laid out through a particular part of the ſame county the ſaid juſtices are hereby authoriſed and required to order a proper ſurveyor with two other men to repair to the ground pointed out in the ſaid petition and at the proper expenſe of the petitioners to view and ſurvey the ſame truly meaſuring the diſtance noting the ſeveral courſes monumenting and numbering every mile's end and conſpicuouſly marking or blazing the trees through the whole length of the way and erecting monuments where there ſhall happen to be no trees which ſurvey ſo made ſhall be reported to the next ſeſſions of the court and if no ſufficient objections to ſuch propoſed high-way are preſented to the ſaid court at the ſame ſeſſions to which ſuch report ſhall be made then the juſtices aforeſaid ſhall on the laſt day of their ſitting in ſuch ſeſſions cauſe ſuch report to be entered of record filing at the ſame time the original in the office of the clerk of the ſaid court.

Sec. 2. And thereupon the juſtices ſhall order the ſupervifors of the high-ways in the ſeveral townſhips in the ſaid county or of ſuch townſhips as they in their diſcretion may think proper and contiguous thereto to open ſuch high-way in ſuch proportions as the ſaid juſtices may think right and equitable each ſupervifor with the inhabitants of his own townſhip opening and rendering commodious for travelling a given diſtance or proportion aſſigned by the juſtices of the ſaid road or high-way according to the greater or leſs number of citizens in each townſhip whoſe inhabitants may be ordered to aſſiſt in opening the ſaid high-way.

Sec. 3. *And be it enacted* That where objections against the opening of such high-way shall be presented to the said justices in due time as aforesaid they shall appoint three disinterested men of the county who at the proper expense of such objectors or opposers of the proposed high way shall repair to the ground and impartially view and examine the same and according to their best and most candid judgment make report in writing to the said justices at their next succeeding sessions of the propriety or impropriety usefulness or inutility of such road or proposed high-way after the reading and due consideration of which the said justices may proceed according to their judgment and order the said road to be established and laid out according to the prayer of the first petitioners or for that time reject the high-way and dismiss the petition. Proceedings on objection to opening high-ways.

Sec. 4. *And be it further enacted* That the said justices in every county as soon as may be after the publication of this act in the several counties respectively shall proceed in their sessions to appoint once every year a proper number of supervisors or overseers of the high-ways in each and every township in the several counties or districts whose province and duty it shall be to obey the orders of the said justices for the laying out of high-ways whenever such orders shall be given in manner aforesaid. And it shall also be the duty of the said supervisors of the high ways to superintend all public roads and high ways in the township for which they may be assigned supervisors or overseers and keep them in proper repair and fit for the use of travellers and passengers by the labour and assistance of the inhabitants of the township in which they may severally be supervisors. And in case of omission of this their duty each default- Supervisors to be appointed; their duty penalty on neglect [illegible];

penalty on neglect thereof.

ing supervisor of the high-ways shall be liable and subjected to a fine of five dollars for each and every default to be recovered with costs for the use of the township by any person who will prosecute for the same for the purpose of aiding the inhabitants of such town to form causeways and smaller bridges where it may be necessary to hire teams for the drawing of timber therefor which fine shall be inflicted by any justice of the peace to whom complaint is made.

Duty of inhabitants;

Sec. 5. *And be it further enacted* That every male inhabitant of sixteen years of age and upwards on being duly warned to work on the high-ways by the supervisor in the township to which such inhabitant may belong shall repair to the place and at the time by the said supervisor appointed with such utensils and tools as may be ordered him wherewith he is to labour and there abide and obey the direction of such supervisor during the day in opening and repairing the high-way. And this duty every male as aforesaid shall be subject to perform so many days not exceeding ten in each year as may in the opinion of the supervisor be necessary for the opening of new and repairing of old high-ways. Provided always that only an equal number of day's labour shall be exacted from any such citizen all such male inhabitants serving alike either in person or by procuring a good hand to labour in their stead or by their team to the acceptance of the supervisor.

forfeiture on neglect thereof.

Sec. 6. And in case any male inhabitant as aforesaid upon receiving three day's notice thereto by the proper supervisor of the high-way shall neglect or refuse to attend at the time and place which may be appointed as aforesaid or shall waste the day in idleness and inattention to the duty assigned him such delinquent ſhall forfeit and pay to the ſupervifor who warned him to work fifty cents for the ſole benefit of the ſaid ſupervifor for every ſuch default to be recovered with coſts by an action of debt in any court where the ſame may be cognizable and moreover be further liable to work an equal number of days yearly on the high-way with the other male inhabitants of the townſhip in the ſame manner as though no ſuch default had been made. Forfeiture on refuſing, &c to work on the high-way;

Sec. 7. And where the delinquent perſon ſhall happen to be a minor apprentice or ſervant the father guardian or mother of ſuch minor or the maſter of ſuch apprentice or ſervant (as the caſe may be) ſo making default ſhall become liable to the action in the ſame manner as though they were principal defaulters. by whom paid in caſe of minors, &c.

Sec. 8. *And be it enacted* That when in the opinion of the ſaid juſtices it may be neceſſary to have conſtructed and built within the county a bridge or bridges of larger dimenſions and ſuch as cannot be erected but at conſiderable expenſe the building of which would be an unreaſonable burthen to the inhabitants of any townſhip ſingly in ſuch caſe the ſaid juſtices are hereby authoriſed to make an eſtimate of the probable expenſes which will accrue by building ſuch large bridge or bridges as aforeſaid which ſhall be included in the general eſtimate of county charges yearly to be made and ſubmitted to the conſideration of the legiſlature. Expenſe of bridges how defrayed.

Signed WINTHROP SARGENT
JOHN CLEVES SYMMES
RUFUS PUTNAM.

CHAPTER V.

An ACT *directing the building and establishing of a Court-house County Jail Pillory Whipping-post and Stocks in every county. Passed at Cincinnati in the county of Hamilton the first day of August in the year of our Lord one thousand seven hundred and ninety two by* Winthrop Sargent *Secretary now vested with all the powers of the Governour and* John Cleves Symmes *and* Rufus Putnam *Judges.*

Court-houses to be erected and established in each county;

Sec. 1. BE *it enacted* That as soon as provision can be made therefor agreeably to "An Act directing the manner in which money shall be raised and levied to defray the charges which may arise within the several counties in the territory" there shall be erected and established in each and every county not having the same already established therein a good and convenient court-house for the legal adjudication of causes and a strong and sufficient common jail or prison for the reception and confinement of debtors and criminals well secured by timber iron bars grates bolts and locks and also a pillory whipping-post and so many stocks as may be convenient for the punishment of offenders and every jail so to be erected shall consist of two apartments one of which shall be appropriated to the reception of the debtors and the other shall be used for the safe keeping of persons charged with or convicted of crimes.

of what materials and dimensions;

Sec. 2. *And be it enacted* That every court-house and jail to be erected as aforesaid shall be formed of such materials and to such dimensions and on such plans as shall be directed by the judges of the county Court of Common Pleas or a majority of them in each county who are hereby authorised to plan and project the same and to accept as a gift or to purchase for the use of the county so much ground as they may judge convenient and neceſſary whereon to build all or any of the ſtructures aforeſaid which purchaſe money ſhall be defrayed by the county and laid in the eſtimate hereafter directed to be made.

Sec. 3. *And be it enacted* That the ſaid judges of the Common Pleas or a majority of them in each and every county ſhall appoint two commiſſioners of induſtry and knowledge ſufficient to plan and execute the work neceſſary for carrying this law into effect by drawing the draught ſuperintending the foundation and erecting and completing of ſuch court-houſe jail pillory whipping-poſt and ſeveral ſtocks reſpectively and for the faithful diſcharge of their duty in this behalf the ſaid commiſſioners ſhall enter into bonds of two hundred dollars with ſufficient ſureties to the judges of the Common Pleas in truſt for the county well and truly to account with the ſaid judges as often as they may thereunto be required by them for the diſpoſition of all money and other property by them received from time to time from the judges or the treaſurer of the county or from any other perſon or by any means whatever for the purpoſe of aiding or aſſiſting in building the ſaid court-houſe jail and other ſtructures in the county to which the commiſſioners may ſeverally belong and on default in the commiſſioners for want of attention or competent knowledge to carry on the work with propriety the ſaid judges ſhall have power to diſcharge one or both of them and place others in their ſtead taking the ſame ſurety from them.

Commiſſioners to be appointed to ſuperintend the building of them; to give bond.

Sec. 4. *And be it alſo enacted* That every county now or hereafter to be erected and laid off within the ſaid territory ſhall defray all expenſes that may attend the building and keeping in good and ſufficient repair within it-

Each county to defray expenſe of court-houſe, &c.

In what cases judges shall draw money, &c.

ſelf the court-houſe jail pillory whipping-poſt and ſtocks hereby ordered and to this purpoſe for the greater forwarding of the buſineſs it ſhall be lawful for the judges aforeſaid and they are hereby authoriſed to draw out of the hands of the treaſurer of the county any ſums of money which he may have received belonging to the county not otherwiſe appropriated and the ſaid judges are hereby directed to apply the ſame wholly to the purpoſes of making preparations for and advances towards building the ſaid court-houſe and jail but in every county where there is no jail already provided the judges ſhall firſt appropriate all the monies they may draw from the treaſurer towards building and finiſhing a proper jail for the reception of debtors and criminals. And the treaſurer of each and every county is hereby authorized and directed to pay to the ſaid judges or on their order to the commiſſioners any ſum or ſums of money which he may have received belonging to the county and not otherwiſe appropriated always taking duplicate receipts for all payments by him made to the judges or to the ſaid commiſſioners by order of the judges one of which receipts the treaſurer ſhall lodge with the clerk of the Court of General Quarter Seſſions.

Money for erecting court-houses how to be provided.

Sec. 5. *And be it enacted* That in order to make ſufficient proviſion in each county of labour money and proper materials neceſſary for the ſeveral purpoſes aforeſaid the juſtices of the Court of General Quarter Seſſions of the Peace or a majority of them in each county ſhall make out an eſtimate of the probable expenſes attending the carrying into effect the aforeſaid ſeveral buildings and ſhall lay the ſame before the governour and judges of the territory as ſoon as may be after ſuch eſtimate can be made that the legislature may direct the raising of the same or such part thereof as they may deem necessary.

Signed WINTHROP SARGENT
JOHN CLEVES SYMMES
RUFUS PUTNAM.

CHAPTER VI.

An ACT *for the better regulation of Prisons passed at Cincinnati in the county of Hamilton the first day of August in the year of our Lord one thousand seven hundred and ninety-two by* Winthrop Sargent *Secretary and now vested with all the powers of the Governour and* John Cleves Symmes *and* Rufus Putnam *Judges.*

Sec. 1. BE *it enacted* That where the escape of any prisoner in a civil or qui-tam action shall happen through the insufficiency of the jail or the negligence of the sheriff or jailer the sheriff of the county in which the escape happens shall stand chargeable to the plaintiff creditor or other person at whose suit or for whose debt he or she was committed or to whose use any forfeiture was adjudged against such prisoner. In what cases the sheriff shall be liable on escape of prisoner;

Sec. 2. And in case the escape shall happen through the insufficiency of the jail the Court of Common Pleas in the county shall have power and authority hereby to assess the sum or sums for which such prisoner stood committed upon the inhabitants of the county in the same manner as is directed by the act entitled " An Act directing the manner in which money shall be raised and levied to defray the charges which may arise within the several counties in the territory" and to order the county treasurer to pay the same when collected to the sheriff of the county that the sheriff may be indemnified. and county assessed for amount of the debt.

In what cases sheriff may bring action against a county.

Sec. 3. And if the Court of Common Pleas ſhall not cauſe ſuch aſſeſſment to be made and if the treaſurer ſhall not pay ſuch ſum or ſums of money within ſix months next after the demand ſhall be laid before the ſaid court then the ſheriff of the county may bring his action againſt the inhabitants of ſuch county to be heard and tried either in that or in one of the adjoining counties at the election of the plaintiff and an atteſted copy of the writ being left (thirty days before the ſitting of the court where the action is brought) with the county treaſurer by the coroner of the ſame county ſhall be held and adjudged to be ſufficient and legal ſervice of the writ and notice of the ſuit. And the juſtices of the Court of General Quarter Seſſions of the Peace ſhall have full power to appoint an agent or attorney to appear on behalf of the county and defend ſuch action and if judgment ſhall be given againſt the county the contents thereof may be raiſed by execution levied upon the monies belonging to the county and then in the hands of the county treaſurer which ſhall be made manifeſt by the ſaid treaſurer's books for which purpoſe the officer having the execution ſhall have leave of the treaſurer in his preſence to peruſe his books and examine his accounts with the county and if the county funds then in the hands of the treaſurer ſhall be found inſufficient to diſcharge the execution and coſts thereon then ſo much of the monies which the treaſurer may next afterwards receive belonging to the county as may be neceſſary to diſcharge the balance on the execution and coſts ſhall be and are hereby pledged attached and bound by virtue of ſuch execution and ſhall be immediately paid over by the treaſurer ſo ſoon as they come to his hands until ſuch execution be fully diſcharged.

Sec. 4. *And be it further enacted* That if any person or persons shall directly or indirectly by any ways or means howsoever without the knowledge or privity of the keeper convey any instrument tool or other thing whatsoever to any prisoner or into any prison whereby any prisoner might break the prison or work himself or herself unlawfully out of the same every person so offending shall forfeit and pay such fine as by the direction of the court shall be imposed not exceeding one hundred dollars according to the nature of the cause of the prisoner's commitment or suffer such corporal punishment not exceeding forty stripes as the court shall inflict and if it shall so happen that any prisoner shall make his or her escape by means of any instrument tool or other thing so conveyed without the knowledge and privity of the keeper the person so conveying the same shall be liable to pay all such sums of money as the prisoner stood committed for if on civil process and shall also have inflicted upon him or her all such punishment as the escaped prisoner would be liable unto if a criminal and had been convicted of the charge for which he or she had been committed unless such prisoner would be liable to capital punishment in which case the person assisting in such escape shall be punished by fine imprisonment whipping pillory or setting on the gallows with a rope about his or her neck or any one or more of the said punishments as the court having cognizance thereof shall think proper to inflict.

Persons aiding in escape of prisoners how punished.

Sec. 5. *And be it further enacted* That if any jailer or prison-keeper shall voluntarily suffer any prisoner committed unto him to escape he shall suffer and undergo the like pains punishment and penalties as the prisoner so escaping should or ought by law to have suffered and

In what case jailer to be liable for punishment due the prisoner.

In what case jailer to be liable for punishment due the prisoner;

undergone for the crime or crimes wherewith he stood charged if he had been convicted thereof. And if any jailer or prison-keeper shall through negligence suffer any prisoner accused of any crime to escape he shall pay such fine as the justices of the court before whom he is convicted shall in their discretion inflict according to the nature of the offence for which the escaped prisoner stood committed.

Sec. 6. *Provided nevertheless* That if any person who may be committed for debt shall violently escape from prison without connivance of the sheriff or keeper and the sheriff the jailer or the prison-keeper shall within three months next after such escape recover the prisoner so escaped and recommit him to prison again then the sheriff shall be liable to nothing farther than the costs of such action or actions as may have been commenced against him for such escape.

duty of sheriff and jailer herein;

Sec. 7. *And be it further enacted* That all warrants mittimuses writs and instruments of writing of any kind or the attested copies of them by which any prisoner may be committed enlarged or liberated shall be safely kept (regularly filed in their order of time) in a suitable box for the purpose provided by the keeper of the jail under the sheriff's direction and upon the death or removal of any sheriff the box with the contents thereof shall be delivered to his successor in the office on the penalty of one hundred and fifty dollars to be paid by the sheriff removed or his executors or administrators in case of the death of the sheriff to be recovered by any person who shall prosecute therefor to effect in any court having jurisdiction to try the same.

Sec. 8. And it ſhall be the duty of the ſaid juſtices at the beginning of every Court of Quarter Seſſions of the Peace to enquire into the ſtate of the priſons in their reſpective counties with regard to the ſufficiency of ſuch priſons the condition and accommodation of the priſoners and ſhall from time to time take ſuch legal meaſures as may beſt tend to ſecure the priſoners from eſcape ſickneſs and infection and to have the jails cleanſed from filth and vermin.

duty of juſtices herein.

Sec. 9. The ſheriff ſhall keep ſeparate rooms for the ſexes except where they are lawfully married and be reſponſible that his jailer at all times provide proper meat and drink for all criminals committed to the priſon of the county if ſuch priſoners have no other convenient way of ſupplying themſelves with proviſions which ſhall always paſs to them through the keeper's hands and in every caſe where the ſheriff or jailer ſhall be at the expenſe of furniſhing meat drink or fire-wood to a priſoner in jail for a crime or at the ſuit of the United States who is not of ſufficient ability in point of property to repay or indemnify ſuch ſheriff or jailer their reaſonable expenſe and charges for ſupplying ſuch priſoner in every ſuch caſe the ſheriff or jailer ſhall make out his account thereof and on oath ſhall teſtify the truth of the ſame before the juſtices of the Court of General Quarter Seſſions of the Peace who ſhall tax the ſame as they ſhall think juſt and reaſonable and lay the amount thereof in the yearly eſtimate of county charges to be ſubmitted to the legiſlature for their allowance.

Sheriff to keep ſeparate rooms for the ſexes, &c.

Sec. 10. *And be it enacted* That in every caſe where any perſon is committed to priſon in a civil action either on meſne proceſs or in execution for debt treſpaſs ſlander or other

Sheriff to provide certain food.

Sheriff to provide certain food, &c.

cause of action at the suit of one citizen against another or at the suit of an alien ally against a citizen or at the suit of a citizen against an alien ally in every such case it shall be the duty of the sheriff to provide only the daily bread and water of such prisoner and he is hereby directed to furnish the same regularly to every such prisoner who is not of sufficient ability in point of property to provide for his or her own support while in prison and the expense and charges accruing to the sheriff or jailer herein shall be repaid to him by the prisoner so soon as the prisoner shall be liberated from the jail for the recovery of which the sheriff or jailer shall have his action at law against the prisoner in any court where the same may be cognizable and when any prisoner shall be committed to jail in a civil action as aforesaid and shall provide for his or her own support in a way wherein the sheriff or jailer shall have no concern it shall be the duty of the jailer or prison-keeper to admit to the wicket grate or small window of the prison in which such prisoner shall be confined any person who may come to administer to the wants of such prisoner by furnishing him or her with meat and drink which shall be conveyed through such small window or grate that the security of the prison be not too frequently exposed by opening the doors thereof.

Disposition of the fines and penalties herein.

Sec. 11. *And be it enacted* That all fines and penalties arising upon the breach of this act shall be for the use of the county where the offence is committed or the duty neglected and the same remedy shall be had for the recovery thereof as in other cases where duties are enjoined by statute and no particular mode of prosecution directed. In cases of default it shall be the duty of the attorney prosecuting the pleas of the United States to prosecute for the same either by writ or on indictment and the fine when recovered shall be paid to the county treasurer for the use of the county.

Signed
WINTHROP SARGENT
JOHN CLEVES SYMMES
RUFUS PUTNAM.

CHAPTER VII.

An ACT *for the disposition of Strays passed at Cincinnati the first day of August in the year of our Lord one thousand seven hundred and ninety-two by* Winthrop Sargent *Secretary now vested with all the powers of the Governour and* John Cleves Symmes *and* Rufus Putnam *Judges.*

Sec. 1. BE *it enacted and it is hereby enacted* That the open woods and uninclosed grounds within the territory shall be taken and considered as the common pasture or herbage of the citizens thereof saving to all persons their right of fencing. Grounds considered as common pasture.

Sec. 2. And if any person after the first day of March and before the first day of December yearly and every year shall take up or confine lead ride or drive away any domestic animal of any kind running in the uninclosed grounds of the territory and committing no trespass he she or they so taking up or molesting such beast unless such animal be previously advertised by the owner as a stray shall forfeit and pay to the owner of the beast ten per cent. on the value of the said beast which valuation shall be made by the judge or jury before whom the cause is tried and moreover return the animal to the owner without delay and the owner shall have an action in replevin for the beast and shall also recover such further damages and costs as the court may adjudge where the action is brought and the court shall award execution accordingly. In certain cases forfeiture on confining domestic animals, &c.

In what cafes perfons riding, &c. domeftic animals fhall be punifhed.

Sec. 3. And if any perfon or perfons fhall prefume to take up and lead ride or drive away any beaft running in uninclofed grounds as aforefaid and fhall convey the fame out of the county fuch perfon fo offending fhall be indicted therefor at the fuit of the United States and on conviction fhall fuffer fuch imprifonment fine or corporal punifhment (not extending to life or limb) as the juftices of the court fhall inflict and fhall alfo pay to the owner of the beaft when known double the value of the fame together with cofts of fuit to be recovered in any court where cognizable.

Proceedings to be had on beafts breaking into enclofures.

Sec. 4. And whenever any beaft fhall break into any enclofure furrounded by lawful fence the owner of fuch field or fome other perfon under his or her authority may take up and fecure the faid beaft agreeably to the act entitled "An Act regulating the enclofures of grounds." And on all fuch occafions the clerk of the townfhip fhall (after raifing damages charges and cofts from the fale of one or more of the beafts agreeably to the aforefaid act) caufe the remaining beafts if any to be turned again into the open woods or commons at all times from the firft day of March to the firft day of December.

When a ftray may be taken up.

Sec. 5. *And be it enacted* That from and after the firft day of December to the firft day of March yearly and every year it fhall be lawful for any citizen of the territory finding horfes or neat cattle running aftray in the woods or commons or trefpaffing for whom there fhall appear no owner living within fix miles of the place to take up and fecure fuch ftray and convey it fo foon as may be done to the clerk of the townfhip in which fuch ftray is found and deliver it to him agreeably to the act entitled "An Act to authorize and require

" the Courts of General Quarter Seſſions of " the Peace to divide the counties into town- " ſhips and to alter the boundaries of the ſame " when neceſſary and alſo to appoint conſtables " overſeers of the poor and clerks of townſhips " and for other purpoſes therein mentioned," for which ſervice the perſon driving ſuch ſtrays to the clerk of the townſhip ſhall be entitled to receive from him on the ſale of the ſtrays five cents on the dollar value of the ſtrays delivered and the clerk ſhall appraiſe the ſame and give a certificate thereof.

Sec. 6. And the clerk of the ſeveral townſhips reſpectively whenever any ſtray ſhall be brought to him ſhall forthwith receive the ſame into his charge and care and provide for its proper keeping and ſupport at as reaſonable a rate as the ſame can be procured and ſhall proceed without delay to advertize agreeably to the laſt mentioned act. And after continuing ſuch advertiſements ſix weeks and no owner appearing to prove property before the neareſt juſtice of the peace and pay charges in ſuch caſe the clerk ſhall proceed to ſell the ſaid ſtray at vendue and on the ſale and delivery of every ſuch beaſt he ſhall give to the purchaſer a certificate thereof deſcriptive of the beaſt with a receipt for the money paid therefor which certificate ſhall be evidence of title for the ſame to the purchaſer. Duty of county clerk in caſes of ſtrays.

Sec. 7. And the clerk of the townſhip ſhall in all caſes have five cents in the dollar value for his ſervices if the beaſt be reclaimed before ſale and ten cents in the dollar value if the ſtray be ſold agreeably to law and after deducting his own fees as alſo the charges of keeping the ſtray and the allowance made herein to the perſon bringing in the ſtray the clerk ſhall pay His allowance.

the reſidue of the proceeds of ſale to the treaſurer of the county for the uſe of the county taking his receipt therefor which he ſhall tranſmit to the clerk of the Court of Quarter Seſſions for the county. And on default thereof in the town clerk he ſhall be liable to an action for ſuch ſum with coſts at the ſuit of the county treaſurer in any court where the ſame may be cognizable.

Perſons claiming ſuch aſtrays how to be indemnified.

Sec. 8. And if after ſale as aforeſaid the owner of ſuch ſtray ſhall by tracing out the property diſcover it to have been ſold by the clerk as aforeſaid and the proceeds of ſale depoſited in the hands of the county treaſurer ſuch owner may apply to the juſtices of the Court of Quarter Seſſions and exhibit before them the proofs of title to ſuch ſtray and if in the opinion of the ſaid juſtices ſuch claimant had title in the ſtray at the time of ſale the ſaid juſtices may and are hereby authoriſed to iſſue their order under the hand of the clerk and the ſeal of the court directing the county treaſurer to repay the money that came to his hands by the ſale of ſuch beaſt and the county treaſurer is hereby directed to obey ſuch order.

Part of certain act repealed.

Sec. 9. *And be it further enacted* That ſo much of the act entitled " An Act to authoriſe and require the Court of General Quarter Seſſions of the Peace to divide the counties into townſhips and to alter the boundaries of the ſame when neceſſary and alſo to appoint conſtables overſeers of the poor and clerks of townſhips and for other purpoſes therein mentioned" as is repugnant to this law be and the ſame is hereby repealed.

WINTHROP SARGENT
Signed JOHN CLEVES SYMMES
RUFUS PUTNAM.

CHAPTER VIII.

An ACT *to repeal certain parts of an act entitled an act "creating the office of Clerk of the Legislature" passed at Cincinnati in the county of Hamilton the first day of August in the year of our Lord one thousand seven hundred and ninety-two by* Winthrop Sargent *Secretary now vested with all the powers of the Governour and* John Cleves Symmes *and* Rufus Putnam *Judges.*

WHEREAS the general government has made certain provision for publishing the laws of this territory

Be it therefore enacted That so much of the act entitled "An Act creating the office of clerk of the legislature" as makes it obligatory upon the said clerk to procure and furnish authenticated copies of the laws of this territory to the governour to each of the territorial judges to the several Courts of Common Pleas and Quarter Sessions of the Peace and judges of probate be and the same is hereby repealed. Act creating clerk to the legislature repealed

Signed
WINTHROP SARGENT
JOHN CLEVES SYMMES
RUFUS PUTNAM.

CHAPTER IX.

An ACT *supplementary to a law entitled a "Law regulating Marriages" passed at Cincinnati in the county of Hamilton and Territory of the United States north west of the river Ohio the first day of August in the year of our Lord one thousand seven hundred and ninety-two by* Winthrop Sargent *Secretary now vested with all the powers of the Governour and* John Cleves Symmes *and* Rufus Putnam *Judges.*

BE *it enacted by the authority aforesaid* That from and after passing this act each and every justice of the peace shall and he is hereby authorized and empowered to solemnize marriages within his own county on the bans being duly published and certified agree- Justices empowered to solemnize marriages.

ably to the aforeſaid law or by ſpecial licenſe from the governour.

Signed — WINTHROP SARGENT
JOHN CLEVES SYMMES
RUFUS PUTNAM.

CHAPTER X.

An ACT *to regulate the admiſſion of Attornies paſſed at Cincinnati county of Hamilton Territory of the United States north-weſt of the river Ohio the firſt day of Auguſt Anno Domini one thouſand ſeven hundred and ninety-two by* Winthrop Sargent *Secretary now veſted with all the powers of the Governour and* John Cleves Symmes *and* Rufus Putnam *Judges.*

Attornies how to be admitted to practice.

Sec. 1. BE *it enacted* That from and after the firſt day of January next no perſon ſhall be admitted or practiſe as an attorney in any of the courts of this territory unleſs he is a perſon of good moral character and well affected to the government of the United States and of this territory and ſhall paſs an examination of his profeſſional abilities before one or more of the territorial judges and obtain from him or them before whom he may be examined a certificate of poſſeſſing the proper abilities and qualifications to render him uſeful in the office of an attorney. And further ſhall in open court have taken and ſubſcribed the oath preſcribed to all officers by an act of the United States and an oath in tenor following

To take oath.

" I ſwear that I will do no falſehood nor
" conſent to the doing of any in the courts of
" juſtice and if I know of an intention to com-
" mit any I will give knowledge thereof to
" the juſtices of the ſaid courts or ſome of
" them that it may be prevented. I will not
" wittingly or willingly promote or ſue any
" falſe groundleſs or unlawful ſuit nor give

"aid or consent to the same and I will con-
"duct myself in the office of an attorney with-
"in the said courts according to the best of
"my knowledge and discretion and with all
"good fidelity as well to the courts as my
"clients. So help me God."

Sec. 2. *And it is enacted* That parties may plead and manage their own causes personally or by the assistance of such counsel as they shall see fit to engage but the plaintiff or plaintiffs in any suit shall not be allowed to manage their cause by more than two attornies nor shall any defendant employ a greater number. Provided that where there shall be only two attornies attending the courts in any of the counties of this territory neither the plaintiff nor defendant shall be allowed more than one nor in any cause shall fees for more than one attorney be taxed or allowed. Parties may manage their own causes.

Signed
WINTHROP SARGENT
JOHN CLEVES SYMMES
RUFUS PUTNAM."

CHAPTER XI.

An ACT *empowering the Judge of Probate to appoint Guardians to Minors and others passed at Cincinnati in the county of Hamilton by* Winthrop Sargent *Secretary vested with all the powers of the Governour of the Territory and* John Cleves Symmes *and* Rufus Putnam *Judges the first day of August in the year of our Lord one thousand seven hundred and ninety-two.*

Sec. 1. BE *it enacted* That the judge of probate in each county respectively when and so often as there shall be occasion be and hereby is empowered to allow of guardians that shall be chosen by minors of fourteen years of age and to appoint guardians for such as shall be within or under that age taking sufficient security of such guardians for the faith- Proceedings to be had in the appointing of guardians.

Guardians how to be appointed.

ful discharge of their trust and to account either with the judge or minor when such minor shall arrive at the age of twenty-one years or at such other time as the judge upon complaint made to him shall direct and when any minor above the age of fourteen years shall be cited by the judge of probate to choose a guardian and such minor shall refuse or neglect to appear or when appearing shall refuse to choose a guardian or any guardian chosen by such minor shall be unable to give sufficient security or shall refuse the trust in every such case the judge of probate shall have the same power to appoint a guardian as though such minor was under the age of fourteen years. Provided nevertheless that when a minor above the age of fourteen years shall choose a guardian such minor may have that choice certified to the judge by a justice of the peace in the same county or by the town clerk which choice so certified shall be deemed as good and valid as if done in the said judge's presence.

Power of judges of probate.

Sec. 2. *And be it further enacted* That it shall be in the power of the judges of the probate of wills within their respective counties from time to time (upon request made by the friends or relations of any ideot non compos or lunatic person or by any overseer of the poor in the town where such ideot non compos or lunatic lives or is an inhabitant) by his writ to direct the sheriff of the county to summon twelve freeholders good and discreet men of the same township to make inquisition thereinto and if the person said to be an ideot lunatic or distracted person shall be adjudged by such inquest (or the major part of them) to be incapable to take care of him or herself and they shall certify the same under their hands to the judge the said judge of probate shall be empowered to aſſign ſome ſuitable perſon or perſons to be guardian or guardians to ſuch ideot lunatic non compos or diſtracted perſon directing and empowering ſuch guardian or guardians to take care of the perſon and eſtate both real and perſonal of ſuch perſon and to make a true and perfect inventory of the ſaid eſtate to be returned into and filed in the probate office of ſuch county.

Sec. 3. *And be it further enacted* That the guardian or guardians appointed as aforeſaid ſhall improve frugally and without waſte or deſtruction the eſtate of the ideot non compos lunatic or diſtracted perſon and apply the annual income and profits thereof for the comfortable maintenance and ſupport of the ſaid ideot non compos lunatic or diſtracted perſon and alſo of his or her houſehold or family (if any ſuch there be) and the ſaid guardian or guardians are hereby empowered to ſettle accounts receive (and if need be) to ſue for and recover all juſt debts due to the ſaid ideot lunatic non compos or diſtracted perſon from any perſon or perſons whomſoever and to manage improve or divide the real eſtate in as full and ample a manner as the ſaid ideot lunatic non compos or diſtracted perſon might or could were they reſtored to the full uſe of their rational faculties and ſhall alſo be ſubject to the payment of all juſt debts owing by ſuch perſon which were contracted before his or her diſtraction out of their perſonal eſtate or in caſe that be inſufficient then out of the real eſtate in ſuch way and manner as executors or adminiſtrators may or ſhall by law be enabled to diſcharge the debts of deceaſed perſons when the perſonal eſtate of ſuch deceaſed perſons ſhall be found inſufficient. And in caſe any ſuch ideot lunatic or diſtracted perſon ſhall be re-

Duty of guardians.

Power.

ſtored to the uſe of his or her reaſon the reſidue and remainder of the eſtate real and perſonal ſhall be returned and delivered to him or her and in caſe of his or her death to his or her heirs executors or adminiſtrators the guardian or guardians having firſt ſuch a reaſonable allowance out of the ſame for their charge and trouble as the judge of probate ſhall order.

Guardians to give bond.

Sec. 4. *And be it further enacted* That the guardian or guardians appointed as aforeſaid ſhall give bond to the judge of probate for the time being in a reaſonable ſum with ſufficient ſureties for the faithful diſcharge of the truſt repoſed in them and more eſpecially for the rendering a juſt and true account of their guardianſhip when and ſo often as they ſhall be thereunto required.

In what caſes judges may appoint guardians.

Sec. 5. *And be it further enacted* That the judges of probate in their reſpective counties may alſo as occaſion may require appoint guardians for the children of lunatics ideots non compos or diſtracted perſons in the ſame way and manner as though their parents were naturally dead. And whereas to the diſhonour of human nature and the great injury of ſociety individuals often times ſpend leſſen and waſte their eſtates by exceſſive drinking gaming idleneſs and debauchery and thereby involve themſelves and families in diſtreſs miſery and ruin and ſubject the town or county to which they belong to expenſe and charge for their maintenance and ſupport.

Duty of overſeers on perſons waſting their eſtates &c.

Sec. 6. *Be it therefore enacted* That when any perſon by exceſſive drinking gaming idleneſs or debauchery of any kind ſhall ſo ſpend waſte or leſſen his or her eſtate as thereby to expoſe himſelf or herſelf or his or her family or any of them to want or ſuffering circumſtances or ſhall by thus ſpending waſting or leſſening his or her eſtate endanger or expoſe the Town or County to which he or ſhe belongs (in the judgment of the overſeers of the poor thereof) to charge and expenſe for the maintenance or ſupport of him or her or his or her family or any of them it ſhall be the duty of the overſeers or overſeer of the poor of the Town to which ſuch perſon belongs (more eſpecially if any of the friends or relations of ſuch perſon ſhall requeſt it of them) in ſuch caſe to lodge a complaint with the judge of probate for the County to which the perſon ſpending waſting or leſſening his eſtate as aforeſaid doth belong. And if it ſhall appear to the judge of probate and two of the judges of the Common Pleas whom he ſhall call to his aſſiſtance that the perſon complained of comes within the deſcription of this act and has had due notice of the complaint exhibited againſt him or her as the caſe may be then and in that caſe the ſaid judge of probate ſhall appoint ſome ſuitable and diſcreet perſon or perſons guardian or guardians to ſuch perſon. And no ſale or bargain of any real or perſonal eſtate made by ſuch perſon or perſons after the appointment of guardianſhip as aforeſaid ſhall be held valid in law nor ſhall he or ſhe be able to contract any debt or make any aſſumption. And the guardian or guardians that may be thus appointed ſhall in diſcharging the duties of their appointment have the ſame authority purſue the ſame method and be under ſimilar obligation for a faithful diſcharge of their truſt as guardians appointed for ideots lunatics or perſons non compos mentis.

Duty of overſeers on perſons waſting their eſtates.

Sec: 7. *And be it further enacted* That executors adminiſtrators and guardians ſhall not be compelled to plead ſpecially to any action or

Executors, &c. not to plead ſpecially to any action,

ſuit at law brought againſt them in their ſaid capacity but may under the general iſſue give any ſpecial matter in evidence.

Signed WINTHROP SARGENT
JOHN CLEVES SYMMES
RUFUS PUTNAM.

CHAPTER XII.

An ACT *preſcribing forms of writs in civil cauſes and directing the mode of proceeding therein paſſed at Cincinnati the firſt day of Auguſt in the year of our Lord one thouſand ſeven hundred and ninety-two by* Winthrop Sargent *Secretary now veſted with all the powers of the Governour of the Territory and* John Cleves Symmes *and* Rufus Putnam *Judges.*

Writs to be in name of United States, &c.

Sec. 1. BE *it enacted* That all writs and proceſs iſſuing from the Court of Common Pleas in the ſeveral Counties ſhall be in the name of the United States and bear teſt of the firſt judge who is not a party and be under the ſeal of the Court and ſigned by the Prothonotary thereof and ſhall have force be obeyed and executed in the proper County where iſſued. And every original proceſs in the Court of Common Pleas ſhall be by ſummons capias or replevin which ſhall be ſerved on the defendant four days before the ſetting of the Court where they are returnable.

Sec. 2. *And be it further enacted* That in all civil actions the original proceſs in the following caſes between party and party ſhall be made out in the forms following: That is to ſay the form of ſummons ſhall be—

Form of ſummons.

(Seal) " Territory of the United States North-
" Weſt of the river Ohio —— Coun-
" ty ſs.
" The United States to the ſheriff of
" our ſaid County of —— Greeting"

" We command you that you ſummon A. B.
" of ſaid County (addition here) if he may be
" found in your bailiwick to appear before our
" judges of our County Court of Common Pleas
" to be holden at ——— in and for our ſaid
" County of ——— on the ——— Tueſday of
" ——— next then and there in our ſaid Court
" to anſwer to C. D. late of ——— (addition)
" in a plea of ——— to the damage of the ſaid
" C. D. as he ſaith the ſum of ——— dollars
" which ſhall then and there be made to appear
" with other damages and of this writ make due
" return.

" Witneſs E. F. Eſquire firſt judge of our
" ſaid Court at ——— the ——— day
" of ——— in the year of our Lord ———
H. I. Prothonotary"

The form of a Capias or Attachment of the perſon ſhall be in the words following viz Form o. capias.

(Seal) " Territory of the United States North-
" Weſt of the river Ohio ——— Coun-
" ty ſs
" The United States to the ſheriff of
" our ſaid county of ——— Greeting
" We command you to take into your cuſtody
" the body of A. B. of ſaid County (addition)
" if he may be found in your bailiwick and
" him ſafely keep ſo that you have ——— be-
" fore our Judges of our County Court of Com-
" mon Pleas next to be holden at ——— within
" and for our ſaid County on the ——— Tueſ-
" day of ——— next then and there in our ſaid
" Court to anſwer unto C. D. late of ———
" (addition) in a plea of ——— to the damage of
" the ſaid C. D. as he ſaith the ſum of ———
" dollars which ſhall then and there be made to
" appear with other damages and of this writ
" make due return. Witneſs E. F. Eſquire, firſt

" Judge of our ſaid Court at —— the —— day
" of —— in the year of our Lord ——
" H. I. Prothonotary."

Form of writ of replevin. The form of a writ of replevin to be iſſued out of the County Court of Common Pleas.

(Seal) " Territory of the United States North-
" Weſt of the river Ohio —— Coun-
" ty ſs.
" The United States to the Sheriff of
" ſaid County of —— Greeting.

" Whereas A. B. of —— (addition) before the judges of our County Court of Common Pleas in and for ſaid County hath ſet up —— title to and property in a certain (here deſcribe with certainty the article or thing to be replevied) which is wrongfully taken and withheld from the ſaid A. B. and is now in the poſſeſſion of C. D. of (addition) as is ſaid.

" Theſe are therefore to require and command you upon ſight hereof to replevy and take into your cuſtody charge and keeping the ſaid (here deſcribe again the things to be replevied) if to be found in your bailiwick and the ſame at all times have ready as you may hereafter be directed by the Judges of our ſaid Court to deliver to the ſaid A. B. in caſe —— ſhall eſtabliſh —— property in and claim thereto in our ſaid Court to be held at —— on the —— Tueſday in —— next. You are alſo hereby commanded to ſummons the ſaid C. D. or ſuch other perſon in whoſe poſſeſſion the ſaid (here deſcribe the articles again) may be found to appear before our ſaid Judges at our ſaid Court at the time and place for holding their next term as aforeſaid and put in —— plea whereby the ſaid C. D. or other perſon may ſhew if any thing they have to ſhew to the contrary of the claim of the aforeſaid A. B. Hereof fail not and of

" this writ make due return at said Court to- " gether with your proceedings herein."

" Witness E. F. Esquire first Judge of our " said Court at —— the —— day of " —— in the year of our Lord ——"

" H. I. Prothonotary."

The FORM of a WRIT of EXECUTION, viz.

Writ of execution.

(Seal) " Territory of the United States north- " west of the river Ohio ——— Coun- " ty, ss.

" The United States to the sheriff of our " said county of ——— Greeting

" Whereas A. B. late of ——— (addition) by " the consideration of our Judges of our Coun- " ty Court of Common Pleas holden at —— for " and within our said County on the —— Tues- " day of —— last recovered judgment against " C. D. of —— (addition) for the sum of —— " dollars —— cents (debt or damages) toge- " ther with —— dollars —— cents costs of " suit as to us appears of record in our said " Court whereof execution remains to be done. " We command you therefore that of the goods " and chattels of the said C. D. within your " bailiwick you cause distress to be made and " thereof levy and pay unto the said A. B. the " aforesaid sums being —— dollars —— cents " in the whole with —— cents more for this " writ and thereof also to satisfy yourself your " own fees and for want of goods or chattels of " the said C. D. to be by —— shewn unto you " or found within your bailiwick we command " you to take the body of the said C. D. and " —— commit to our jail in said County and " —— detain in your custody within our said " jail until —— pay the full sums above men- " tioned with your own fees or that —— be " discharged by the said A. B. the creditor or " otherwise by order of law. Hereof fail not

" and of this writ make due return with your
" proceedings therein unto our said Court at
" the next term to be held at ——— in and for
" said County on the ——— day of ——— next
" ensuing.

" Witness E. F. first Judge of our said Court
" the ——— day of ——— in the year of our
" Lord ———

" H. I. Prothonotary."

Precepts to be in name of United States.

Sec. 3. *And be it further enacted* That all precepts issued by a Judge of the Common Pleas for the trial of small causes shall be in the name of the United States and shall be under the seal of such judge and signed by him and shall have force and be executed in the county where such judge resides and all original process issued by a judge for the trial of small causes shall be by summons or capias which shall be served and executed five days before the day therein set for the trial and not more than twelve days. And the forms of the several precepts in the following cases shall be as follows that is to say.

A SUMMONS

Form of summons;

(*Seal*) " Territory of the United States North-
" west of the river Ohio ——— Coun-
" ty ss.
" To the constable of the town of ———
" or to any or either of the constables of
" said county ——— Greeting.

" In the name of the United States you are
" hereby required to summon and give notice
" unto C. D. of ——— in the county afore-
" said (addition) if he may be found in your
" precinct that he appear before me E. F. Es-
" quire one of the judges of the court of com-
" mon pleas for the county aforesaid at my
" dwelling-house in ——— on the ——— day
" of ——— at ——— of the clock in the ———
" noon then and there to answer to A. B. of

" —— (addition) in a plea of —— to the da-
" mage of the ſaid A. B. as he ſaith the ſum of
" —— as ſhall then and there be made to ap-
" pear together with other damages and of this
" ſummons with your doings herein you are to
" make true return unto me at or before the
" ſaid day of trial. Dated at —— the ——
" day of —— in the year of our Lord ——."

" E. F."

The Form of a Capias or Warrant, viz. of capias or warrant;

(Seal) " Territory of the United States North-
" weſt of the Ohio —— County ſs.
" To the conſtable of the town of ——
" or to any or either of the conſtables
" in the ſaid county ——Greeting.

" In the name of the United States you are
" hereby reqnired to take the body of C. D. of
" —— (addition) if —— may be found
" in your precinct and —— ſafely keep ſ
" that —— may be had before me E. F.
" Eſquire one of the Judges of the Court of
" Common Pleas for the county aforeſaid at my
" dwelling-houſe in —— on —— the ——
" day of —— at —— of the clock in the
" ——noon then and there to anſwer to A. B.
" of (addition) in a plea of —— to the damage
" of the ſaid A. B. as he ſaith the ſum of ——
" as ſhall then and there appear with other da-
" mages. Hereof fail not and make due return
" of this warrant and of your doings therein
" unto me at or before the ſaid day of trial
" dated at the —— day of —— in the year
" of our Lord ——."

" E. F."

The Form of an Execution. of execution

(Seal) " Territory of the United States North-
" weſt of the river Ohio —— Coun-
" ty ſs.

Form of execution.

"The United States to the conſtable of "the town of ——— or to any or ei- "ther of the conſtables of ſaid county " Greeting

"Whereas A. B. of (addition) on the ——— "day of ——— before E. F. Eſquire one of "our Judges of the Court of Common Pleas "for our county aforeſaid recovered judgment "againſt C. D. of (addition) for the ſum of "——— (debt or damage) and ——— for "coſts of ſuit as to us appears of record on the "docket of the ſaid judge whereof execution "remains to be done. We therefore command "you that of the goods and chattels of the ſaid "C. D. within your precinct you cauſe diſtreſs "to be made and thereof levy and pay unto the "ſaid A. B. the aforeſaid ſums being ——— in "the whole and alſo that out of the goods and "chattels of the ſaid C. D. you levy ——— "more for this execution together with your "own fees and for want of ſuch goods or chat- "tels of the ſaid C. D. to be by ——— ſhewn "unto you or found within your precinct We "command you to take the body of the ſaid "C. D. and ——— commit unto our jail in "our ſaid county and we command the keeper "thereof accordingly to receive the ſaid C. D. "into our ſaid jail and ——— therein ſafely "keep until ———pay the full ſums above- "mentioned together with your fees or that "——— be diſcharged by the ſaid A. B. the "creditor or otherwiſe by order of law. Here- "of fail not and of this precept make return "within forty days next coming together with "your doings therein unto our ſaid judge.

"Witneſs E. F. the aforeſaid judge at——— "the ——— day of ——— in the year of "our Lord ———."

"E. F."

Sec. 4. *And be it further enacted* That where the process is by summons the service shall be made by the officers reading the summons in the hearing of the defendant or some of his or her family and giving a copy thereof if demanded and when the party is not to be found by the officer and has no family the service shall be made by the officers leaving an attested copy of the summons at the last and usual place of the defendants abode. And when process is by capias or warrant the service thereof shall be good and legal so far as to oblige the defendant to answer and submit by the officers arresting or attaching the person of the defendant.

Service of summons how to be made.

Sec. 5. *And be it further enacted* That when any defendant shall be duly served with process and return thereof shall be made into the Court where the same is returnable and he or she shall not appear by attorney nor in person to plead within the time ordered by a rule of Court had for the purpose such default shall be recorded and the charge in the declaration shall be taken and deemed to be true and the Court shall thereupon give judgment and assess such damages as they shall find upon enquiry the plaintiff shall have sustained.

Proceedings on default of persons summoned

Provided nevertheless That if the defendant shall come into court before the judge of the pleas for the trial of small causes shall have adjourned his Court or dismissed his suitors or if in the Court of Common Pleas before the jury returned to try the cause is discharged, and shall pay down to the adverse party the costs already accruing or so much thereof as the Court shall judge reasonable then the Court may admit the defendant to have the same day in Court as if such default had never been recorded.

In cases of non suit.

Sec. 6. *And it also enacted* That when any plaintiff shall in any stage of the action become non suit or discontinue the cause the defendant shall recover costs against such plaintiff. And that in all actions as well those of qui tam as others and in all cases the party prevailing shall be entitled to legal costs against the other.

Of persons imprisoned upon mesne process.

Sec. 7. *And be it further enacted* That no person imprisoned upon mesne process shall be held in prison upon such process more than thirty days next after entering up final judgement upon the writ whereby he or she is committed unless he or she shall be continued there by having his or her body taken anew in execution nor shall the prison-keeper discharge any such prisoner unless judgment is given in his or her favour until thirty days next after the said judgment is entered up unless the party at whose suit such prisoner was committed shall give order in writing for the prisoner's discharge and the jailer be paid his legal fees.

Writs how to be endorsed.

Sec. 8. *And be it further enacted* That all original writs issuing out of the Court of Common Pleas shall before they are served be endorsed on the back thereof by the plaintiff or plaintiffs or one of them with his or her name at length if he she or they be inhabitants of the Territory or by his or her agent or attorney being an inhabitant thereof or by some responsible person who is an inhabitant of this Territory. Provided that the Court may upon motion (in consideration that the agent or attorney who endorsed the writ is not of ability for the purpose hereafter mentioned) order that the plaintiff shall procure a new endorser and such new endorser shall be held in the same manner as if the endorsement had been made before the writ was served. And unless the plaintiff shall procure such new endorser when directed thereto by the Court he or she shall become non suit and the plaintiff agent or attorney who shall so endorse his or her name upon an original writ shall be liable (in case of the avoidance or inability of the plaintiff) to pay the defendant all such costs as he or she shall recover and also to pay all prison charges that may happen where the plaintiff fails to support the action.

Sec. 9. *And be it further enacted* That when any action shall be brought to recover a demand or debt due on bond bill note of hand bargain promise book account an account stated by the parties a quantum merruit quantum valebat or for services done upon an agreed price the defendant may file notice of any bond bill note of hand bargain promise assumption or account he or she hath which ought to be set off against the demand of the plaintiff in the clerk's or prothonotary's office seven days before the setting of the Court of Common Pleas where the action is brought or if the suit be before a judge of the Common Pleas in his Court for the trial of small causes the account or other matter pleaded shall be filed before the judge two days before the day of trial and upon the general issue give the same in evidence against the plaintiff's demand. And if upon the trial it shall appear that there is a balance due to the defendant he or she shall recover the same in the same manner as if he or she had brought suit therefor and shall have judgment and execution thereon against the plaintiff and when a plaintiff shall at the same Court bring divers actions which in their nature might have been joined in one he or she shall recover no more costs than in one action only.

Proceedings to be had to recover debts, &c.

Sec. 10. *And be it further enacted* That no summons writ precept declaration process re-

Summons, &c. no to be quashed for want of form.

turn judgment or other proceedings in the Courts or Courſe of Juſtice ſhall be abated arreſted quaſhed reverſed or ſet aſide for any kind of circumſtantial errors or miſtakes when the perſon and caſe, may be rightly underſtood by the Court nor through default or want of form only and the Court on motion may order amendments made therein in aid of juſtice.

When execution ſhall iſſue.

Sec. 11. *And be it further enacted* That execution ſhall not iſſue in any caſe within the juriſdiction of the aforeſaid Courts reſpectively until the expiration of twenty days after entering up of judgment when the party may claim his or her execution or at any time within one year after judgment Provided there be no writ of error certiorari or ſuperſedeas awarded in the cauſe. Provided nevertheleſs that when the party obtaining judgment in any action pending in the ſaid County Court of Common Pleas or in the Court of a Judge of Common Pleas for the trial of ſmall cauſes ſhall make oath (before the ſaid Courts reſpectively) that he or ſhe "verily and truly believes that if execution be ſtayed for the ſpace of twenty days there will be great danger of the debt or contents of the judgment being for ever loſt" in that caſe execution ſhall iſſue immediately.

Proceedings to be had on taking goods, &c.

Sec. 12. *And be it further enacted* That when any goods or chattels ſhall be taken to ſatisfy an execution iſſuing upon a judgment abtained ſuch goods or chattels ſhall be ſafely kept by the officer at the expenſe of the debtor for the ſpace of five days next after they are ſo taken and if within that time the owner or ſome other perſon on his or her behalf ſhall not redeem the ſame by otherwiſe ſatisfying the execution ſuch goods and chattels ſhall be ſold at public vendue to the higheſt bidder having firſt been advertiſed by poſting up notification of the time and place four days before the ſale in the town or place where the ſale is to be. And the money ariſing upon ſuch ſale ſhall be applied to the paying of charges and ſatisfying the execution and the officer levying the ſame ſhall return the overplus (if any there be) to the debtor and ſhall make return of the execution with his doings therein particularly deſcribing the goods taken and ſold and the ſum which each of the articles ſold at. And if any officer ſhall be guilty of any fraud in the ſale or in the return he ſhall be liable to the debtor to pay him three times the ſum defrauded to be recovered by action of the caſe.

Signed
WINTHROP SARGENT
JOHN CLEVES SYMMES
RUFUS PUTNAM.

CHAPTER XIII.

An ACT eſtabliſhing and regulating the Fees of the ſeveral Officers and other perſons therein mentioned paſſed at Cincinnati in the county of Hamilton the firſt day of Auguſt in the year of our Lord one thouſand ſeven hundred and ninety-two by Winthrop Sargent *Secretary now veſted with all the powers of the Governour and* John Cleves Symmes *and* Rufus Putnam *Judges.*

Sec. I. BE *it enacted* That from and after the 1ſt day of January next the fees of the ſeveral officers and other perſons herein after mentioned ſhall be as follows, viz. Fee

JUDGE *of* COMMON PLEAS *in his Court for the trial of ſmall cauſes.* Of J Com Plea

For every precept ſummons warrant capias or writ of attachment to bring the defendant into court. — twenty cents

For the declaration to the perſon drawing the ſame — twenty cents

For a ſubpœna for one or more perſons — ten cents

For ſwearing one or more witneſſes at the ſame time — five cents

Fees.

For entering an action on his docket	five cents
For the trial of an iſſue	twenty cents
For entering up judgment and recording the ſame	twenty cents
For examining allowing and taxing a bill of coſt	five cents
For an execution	twenty-five cents
For a copy of any evidence original paper or record at the rate of for every hundred words.	ſix cents
For a recognizance or bail bond including principal and ſurety	twenty cents

Of juſtice of peace.

JUSTICE *of the* PEACE *in his Court for hearing allegations in criminal matters.*

For every hundred words of an examination taken	ten cents
For hearing a complaint and iſſuing a warrant	twenty cents
For trying an iſſue joined before him	twenty cents
For entering a judgment and recording the ſame	twenty cents
For granting a mittimus	twenty cents
For taking an affidavit out of court in order to be read on the trial of any cauſe	ſix cents
For his travel out in order to take an affidavit and returning from the place per mile.	three cents
For writing a depoſition caption and notification at the rate of for every hundred words.	ten cents
For adminiſtering an oath to one or more witneſſes or other perſons at the ſame time	five cents

For a certificate of an oath administered — five cents

Fees.

For taking the acknowledgment of a deed with one or more seals provided it be at one and the same time and certifying of it — twenty cents

Judge of Probates Fees.

Of judge of probate

For granting a letter of administration — fifty cents
For granting a letter of guardianship — thirty cents
For a decree respecting the probate of a will or codicil — fifty cents
For examining and allowing an inventory and making an entry thereof swearing executors or administrators — twenty cents
For swearing appraisers of an estate where he does it and giving a certificate of the same — ten cents
For examining and allowing an account — thirty cents
A decree for settling intestate estates — thirty cents
For a citation — ten cents
For a summons or subpæna for witnesses — ten cents
For a quietus — fifteen cents
For a warrant to appraise or divide an estate — twenty-five cents
For issuing a commission to receive and examine creditor's claims when estates are represented insolvent — fifteen cents
For an order of distribution — fifteen cents
For granting an appeal to the Court of Probate — fifteen cents

Fees. Of clerk of Orphans Court.

The CLERK *of the* ORPHANS COURT FEES.

For writing a bond and letter of adminiſtration	thirty cents
For writing a bond and letter of guardianſhip and recording the ſame	fifty cents
For drawing a decree reſpecting the probate of a will or codicil	thirty cents
Writing a bond for an executor or adminiſtrator	fifteen cents
For writing a warrant to appraiſe the eſtate of perſons deceaſed	fifteen cents
For writing a warrant ſo divide an inteſtate eſtate among the heirs	fifteen cents
For writing a warrant to ſet off a widow's dower	fifteen cents
For writing a warrant to appoint auditors for examining the claims of an inſolvent eſtate	fiteen cents
For entering on an inventory the oath of the executor and adminiſtrator	five cents
For entering the official account of an executor adminiſtrator or guardian	ten cents
For drawing up a decree on the ſettlement of an eſtate	fifteen cents
For drawing an order of deſtribution agreeable to the will	fifteen cents
For drawing a quietus	fifteen cents
For drawing a citation	ten cents
For drawing a ſummons for a witneſs or witneſſes if he does it	ten cents
For proportioning an inſolvent eſtate among the creditors every creditor's proportion being ſeverally diſtinguiſhed at the rate of every twelve creditors	fifty cents

Fees.

For entering an appeal to the Court of Probate	ten cents
For recording a will inventory or other matter for every hundred words at the rate of	eight cents
For a copy of a will inventory or other papers for every hundred words	ſix cents
For drawing a bond of appeal	fifteen cents

The FEES *in the* COURT *of* PROBATE.

For receiving and entering an appeal to the court	one hundred cents
For giving a final decree to the court	one hundred cents
To the clerk for entering an appeal	ten cents
To the clerk for entering the final decree	ten cents
To the clerk for recording a final decree and all other papers at the rate of for every hundred words	eight cents
To the clerk for all copies for every hundred words.	ſix cents

In the COUNTY COURT *of* COMMON PLEAS

The JUDGES FEES

Of judges in the county court.

On the entry of every action	fifty cents
For every action where an iſſue in fact or law is joined	one hundred cents
For taxing a bill of coſts	ten cents
For taking ſpecial bail	twenty cents
For allowing a writ of error	fifteen cents
For granting a reference	fifteen cents
For approving of the report of referees	fifteen cents
On ſurrender of the principal in court by ſureties	twenty cents

Fees.

For granting a writ of protection	twenty cents
For hearing a petition and making an order thereon	twenty cents
For proving a deed	twenty-five cents
For every order appointing affeffors or refpecting affeffments to be paid by the county	one dollar
For appointing commiffioners to be paid by the county.	two dollars

Of prothonotary of common pleas.

The FEES *of the* PROTHONOTARY *of the* COMMON PLEAS

For every action entered in court	fifteen cents
For entering and recording a verdict or a report of referees	fifteen cents
For every action withdrawn or non fuit	five cents
On every confeffion of judgment default joinder or demurrer	ten cents
For entering up judgment and recording the fame at large	twenty cents
For entering fatisfaction of judgment on record	five cents
For entering allowance to every writ of error	ten cents
For examining each bill of coft	five cents
For every copy of a rule of court	ten cents
For continuing each caufe to the next term	ten cents
For entering the furrender of a principal in court	ten cents
For entering a rule of court upon fubmitting a caufe to referees	ten cents
For every blank writ capias or fummons with the feal of the court	twenty cents
For a blank fcire facias or replevin with the feal annexed	twenty cents

Fees.

For an execution in perſonal matters — twenty-five cents

For every writ of treſpaſs and ejectment — twenty-five cents

For every writ of poſſeſſion in real actions — twenty-five cents

For each warrant for collecting aſſeſſments — twenty cents to be paid by the county.

For making out duplicates of county aſſeſſments to be paid by the county at the rate of — eight cents for every hundred words.

For a venire facias for jurymen in a cauſe traverſed — ten cents

In the COURT *of* GENERAL QUARTER SESSIONS
The JUSTICES FEES.

Of juſtices in court of gen. quarter ſeſſions.

For every recognizanee taken appeal received or granted or writ of certiorari allowed — fifteen cents

On the tri of each cauſe — fifty cents

For every oath adminiſtered in court — five cents

For awarding a mittimus — fifteen cents

For every order paſſed reſpecting the poor high way or other ſervices for the county to be paid out of the county treaſury. — fifteen cents

For every recommendation for a licenſe — one dollar

For taxing a bill of coſts — ten cents

For granting a writ of protection — twenty cents

On ſurrender of the principal in court by ſureties — twenty cents

For hearing a petition and making an order thereon — twenty cents

Fees.

Of clerk of sessions.

The CLERK *of the* SESSIONS FEES.

For entering an indictment complaint or presentment	ten cents
For recording the judgment of court thereon	ten cents
For taking every recognizance or bond therein	fifteen cents
For discharging a recognizance	five cents
For drawing a warrant for apprehending criminals	twenty cents
For each subpœna for one or more witnesses	ten cents
For each recognizance for innholders or retailers	twenty cents
For each order or recommendation for a license including the recording of such license when certified to the sessions by the commissioner	fifteen cents
For reading a petition and entering the order of court thereon	five cents
For examining and casting grand jurors accounts of service and order of court thereon	five cents
For examining any other account	ten cents
For every order for high ways	fifteen cents
For recording every report of a high way accepted by the court at the rate of for every hundred words	eight cents
For entering an appeal or allowance of a writ of certiorari and recognizing the principal and sureties	fifteen cents
For copies of all records or original papers for every hundred words.	six cents

In the GENERAL *or* SUPREME JUDICIAL COURT

Fees. Of judges in supreme court.

JUDGES FEES.

On the entering an action or complaint	one dollar
For taking ſpecial bail	thirty cents
For allowing a writ of error certiorari habeas corpus or other writ of allowance on motion in Court or at his chamber	forty cents
For granting a writ of protection	twenty-five cents
For proving a deed	forty cents
For hearing a petition and making order thereon for the partition of or relating to real eſtates	one dollar
Judgment on partition of real eſtates	thirty cents
For taxing a bill of coſts	fifty cents
For examining and admitting every attorney to practiſe	three dollars
For ſigning a judgment roll	thirty cents
For every oath adminiſtered	five cents
For a writ of ſupercedeas	one dollar
For every juſtification or diſallowance of bail	forty cents

CLERK'S FEES *in the Supreme Judicial Court*

Of clerk in ſupreme court.

For every writ of capias attachment ſcire facias partition replevin ſuperſedeas treſpaſs and ejectment review and every other writ for bringing the defendant into court.	fifty cents
For entering each action on the return of the writ	twenty-five cents
For every complaint entered by him	twenty-five cents

For receiving and recording a verdict fifteen cents
For an execution twenty-five cents
For a writ of facias habere poſſeſſionem fifty cents
For a writ of habeas corpus thirty cents
For copies of all records at the rate of ſix cents for every hundred words.
For entering a rule of court fifteen cents
For entering every confeſſion of judgment default joinder or demurrer fifteen cents
On every action withdrawn or non ſuit fifteen cents
For entering an appearance ten cents
Entering ſatisfaction of a judgment on record ten cents
For examining each bill of coſt ten cents
For continuing each cauſe over and entering the ſame at the next term fifteen cents
For filing each paper two cents
For entering up judgment and recording the ſame at large fifty cents
For every writ with the ſeal of the court affixed other than is before mentioned fifty cents
For each venire facias for jurymen in a traverſe cauſe twenty cents
For every ſubpœna for one or more witneſſes twenty cents
For every recognizance including principal and ſureties twenty cents
For entering a diſcharge of a recognizance by proclamation fifteen cents

In all criminal cauſes his fees ſhall be fifty per centum over and above the allowance or fees given to the clerk of the ſeſſions for the ſame ſervices.

ATTORNIES FEES *to be allowed to the party recovering costs*

Fees. Of attornies.

For a pleading fee when council is employed on an issue in law or fact joined in the Supreme Court two dollars

For all other causes in the Supreme Court and for all causes in the Court of Common Pleas and Court of General Quarter Sessions of the Peace where an issue in fact or law is joined one hundred & fifty cents

And for all other causes in the Common Pleas and Court of Quarter Sessions as a retaining fee one dollar

In criminal causes where one or more defendants are tried by jury at the same time or where a cause is determined by an issue at law a pleading fee for the council in the Supreme Court (but to one counsel) only two dollars

And when no trial is had by jury nor the cause determined by an issue in law one dollar & an half

And in the Court of General Quarter Sessions of the Peace the fees shall be the same as is allowed in the Court of Common Pleas.

To the ATTORNEY *for the* UNITED STATES

Of attorney of United States.

For drawing an indictment in the Sessions fifty cents

For drawing an indictment in the Supreme Court one dollar

For bringing a cause to issue in the Sessions of the Peace fifty cents

For bringing a cause to issue in the General or Supreme Judicial Court one dollar

Fees. For all other ſervices one fourth more than the fees of other attornies for ſimilar ſervices.

To witneſſes.

For the attendance of Witneſſes.

In all civil or criminal cauſes in the Supreme Court Court of Common Pleas and Court of General Quarter Seſſions of the Peace for each days attendance — thirty cents

And three cents for each miles travel going and returning

For each days attendance before a judge of the Pleas in trials of ſmall cauſes or before a juſtice of the Peace — twenty-five cents

per day and the ſame allowance for travel fees as at other courts provided each witneſs do give an account to the clerk or prothonotary of each days attendance and the diſtance travelled.

To coroners.

CORONERS FEES

For ſerving a writ ſummons or execution and for travel in returning the ſame and for returning on an inquiſition the ſame allowance as is by this act allowed to the ſheriff.

For a bail bond in the General Court — thirty cents

For a bail bond in all other courts — fifteen cents

On every trial where the ſheriff ſtands not indifferent — fifteen cents

For attending to the jury — fifteen cents

For granting a venire and taking inquiſition on a dead body — ſeventy-five cents

For his travel and expenſe to take an inquiſition per day — ſeventy-five cents

To the foreman of the jury taking an inquiſition at the rate of per day — ſixty cents

To every other juryman fifty cents per day and for travel of the jurors three cents per mile. Fees.

To a CONSTABLE. To a constable.

For summoning a jury and attendance on a coroner on view of a dead body seventy-five cents per day.

For serving a warrant or capias or summons for each person named therein and served on thirty cents

For a copy of any precept left to complete the service at the rate of six cents for every hundred words.

For serving a subpœna on each person named therein ten cents

For serving an execution twenty-five cents

For attending the vendue for the sale of goods taken in execution fifty cents

To each constable attending a grand jury not more than two at one term forty cents

To the constable attending the jury for the trial of a cause if done by a constable twenty cents

To each constable who shall attend the General or Supreme Judicial Court Common Pleas or Court of Quarter Sessions by their order fifty cents per day to be paid out of the county treasury

SHERIFFS FEES

Sheriff for serving summons.

For the service of an original summons warrant capias attachment scire facias writ of dower writ of ejectment writ

Fees.

of partition and writ of replevin — ſixty cents
for every perſon named in any ſuch writ or proceſs on which the ſame is actually ſerved.

For every copy where the law requires one to be made out to complete the ſervice of any writ or ſummons the ſheriff is allowed — ſix cents
for every hundred words thereof.

For a bail bond and writing the ſame including principal and ſureties — fifteen cents
to be paid by the perſon admitted to bail.

For ſerving a writ of poſſeſſion exclusive of the poundage on the coſts of court — one hundred and ſixty cents
and if on more than one piece of land — eighty cents for each.

For collecting the coſts on a writ of poſſeſſion — the ſame

Poundage as in perſonal actions.

To ſheriffs aid in criminal caſes to each perſon including expenſes for every twelve hours and ſo in proportion for a leſs time — fifty cents

And for each mile travel going out and returning home — three cents
per mile.

For ſerving a ſummons or ſubpœna on witneſſes in criminal caſes — ten cents

For each witneſs ſerved with notice and the ſheriffs travelling fees the ſame as in the ſervice of writs unleſs in ſpecial caſes when the court may increase the same to what they think reasonable. Fees.

For levying execution in personal actions for the first hundred dollars or under five per centum when above one hundred dollars and not exceeding two hundred dollars two and an half per centum and when above two hundred dollars and not exceeding three hundred dollars one and a half per centum and for all above three hundred dollars one per centum. For levying execution.

Travelling fees for the service of any writ summons execution or other process to him directed three cents per mile out the travel to be computed from the place of service to the court where the writ or execution shall be returned by the way that is most commonly used. But one travel only shall be allowed to one writ or execution and if the same be served on more persons than one the travel to be computed from that place of service most remote from the place of return with all further necessary travel in serving such writ or execution the travelling fees of service to be endorsed by the sheriff or his deputy on each mesne process execution or other writ otherwise not to be allowed. Travelling.

For serving execution, &c.

For serving execution upon judgment of court for partition of real estates or for assigning dower	one hundred cents
per day and travel out from the place of his abode three cents per mile.	
For attending every trial in court	ten cents
For attending on a grand jury by his deputy	forty cents
For attending on a traverse jury by his deputy	twenty cents
to be paid with the jurors fees.	
For summoning each traverse	

Fees. jury and returning the panel thereof fifty cents

To each appraiſer of real eſtates for extending execution or aſſigning dower ſeventy-five cents per day and ſo in proportion for a longer or ſhorter time.

Of ſheriff.

CRIERS FEES.

For calling a traverſe jury five cents

On each default non ſuit judgment complaint entered verdict or demurrer ten cents

To the crier for diſcharging a recognizance by proclamation fifteen cents

And all fees allowed the crier ſhall be paid to the clerks of the reſpective courts for the uſe of the crier.

Jailre.

JAILERS FEES.

For turning the key on the commitment of each priſoner fifteen cents in and fifteen cents out.

For dieting each perſon ſuch ſum weekly as the Court of Seſſions ſhall judge reaſonable.

Grand jurors.

GRAND JUROR'S FEES.

To the foreman ſixty cents per day

To each other juror fifty cents per day

For travel in going out and returning home three cents per mile to each juror to be paid out of the county treaſury.

Traverſe jurors.

TRAVERSE JURORS FEES.

To the foreman in every cauſe tried by jury at the Supreme Court Court of Common Pleas and Court of General Seſſions of the Peace twenty cents

And to every other junor ſerving on the jury fifteen cents.

Fees. of Marriages

Fees. Of marriages.

To the town clerk or justice of the peace for publishing the bans of matrimony and making a record thereof twenty-five cents

For every certificate of a publishment ten cents

For each marriage to the minister or magistrate one hundred & ten cents

Fees in the Secretarys Office

For a certificate under the seal of the Territory for the benefit of a particular person one dollar

For every order of notice from the legislature upon petition twelve cents for every hundred words for recording and for all copies eight cents for every hundred words and every other order of the legislature for the benefit of particular persons at the same rate.

For commissions.

For every commission to which fees are annexed under the seal of the Territory one dollar

A commission to a field officer of militia one dollar

A captains commission seventy-five cents

A commission to a subaltern officer fifty cents

County Registers Fees

To count registers.

For entering and recording a deed of partition or other instrument of writing and for certifying on the original the time when the book and page where the same is recorded ten cents for every hundred words thereof the fees to be paid at offering the instrument for registry.

For all copies six cents for every hundred words.

For entering in the margin the discharge of a mortgage to be paid by the person discharging the same fifteen cents

For recording a marriage certified by a minister or a magis-

Fees. trate to be paid by a miniſter or magiſtrate ten cents

Commiſſioners of aſſeſſments.

COMMISSIONERS *of* ASSESSMENTS

For each days attendance when convened on the buſineſs of apportioning the county aſſeſſment on the ſeveral towns and diſtricts fixty cents per day each man

For travelling fees going out and returning home three cents per mile to be paid to them out of the treaſury of the county.

In what caſes paid in kind.

And whereas a dollar varies in its real value in the ſeveral counties of the territory ſome proviſion in kind ought to be made Therefore

Be it enacted That for every cent allowed by this act one quart of Indian corn may be demanded and taken by the perſon to whom the fee is coming, as an equivalent for the cent always at the election of the perſon receiving the ſame whether to accept of his fee in Inian corn or in ſpecie at the ſum affixed by the foregoing table of fees one quart of Indian corn being always equal to one cent and ſo at that rate for a greater or a leſs ſum.

Forfeiture on demanding unlawful fees.

And be it further enacted That if any perſon ſhall demand any greater fee or fees for any of the ſervices aforeſaid than are by this law provided he or they ſhall forfeit and pay for every offence the ſum of ten dollars with coſts of ſuit to the uſe of any perſon who will ſue therefor before any one of the judges of the Court of Common Pleas within one year after ſuch offence is committed.

Signed WINTHROP SARGENT
JOHN CLEVES SYMMES
RUFUS PUTNAM.

A true Copy from the Records by
WINTHROP SARGENT *Secretary*.

www.ingramcontent.com/pod-product-compliance
Lightning Source LLC
Chambersburg PA
CBHW022146090426
42742CB00010B/1416

* 9 7 8 3 3 3 7 3 7 4 4 7 1 *